Ultimate Bi
Diet (

MW01296074

Bikini Competition

Bikini Competitors Guide With Carb Cycling And Clean Eating Recipes To Prepare And Win Your Bikini Fitness Competition!

Sarah Brooks

Copyright © 2015 Sarah Brooks

STOP!!! Before you read any further....Would you like to know the Secrets of Body Transformation?

If your answer is yes, then you are not alone. Thousands of people are looking for the secret to rapidly burn body fat, keep the weight off, become healthier, and truly transform their body and life for good.

If you have been searching for these answers without much luck, you are in the right place!

Not only will you gain incredible insight in this book, but because I want to make sure to give you as much value as possible, right now for a limited time you can get full **100% FREE access to a VIP bonus EBook** entitled **THE 7 KEYS TO BODY TRANSFORMATION!**

Just Go Here For Free Instant Access:

www.liveFitVIP.com

Legal Notice

All rights reserved. Without limiting the rights under the copyright reserved above, no part of this publication may be reproduced, stored in or introduced into a retrieval system, or transmitted, in any form, or by any means (electronic, mechanical, photocopying, recording, or otherwise) without the prior written permission of the copyright owner and publisher of this book. This book is copyright protected. This is for your personal use only. You cannot amend, distribute, sell, use, quote or paraphrase any part or the content within this eBook without the consent of the author or copyright owner. Legal action will be pursued if this is breached.

Disclaimer Notice

Please note the information contained within this document is for educational and entertainment purposes only. Considerable energy and every attempt has been made to provide the most up to date, accurate, relative, reliable, and complete information, but the reader is strongly encouraged to seek professional advice prior to using any of this information contained in this book. The reader understands they are reading and using this information contained herein at their own risk, and in no way will the author, publisher, or any affiliates be held responsible for any damages whatsoever. No warranties of any kind are expressed or implied. Readers acknowledge that the author is not engaging in the rendering of legal, financial, medical, or any other professional advice. By reading this document, the reader agrees that under no circumstances is the author, publisher, or anyone else affiliated with the production, distribution, sale, or any other element of this book responsible for any losses, direct or indirect, which are incurred as a result of the use of information contained within this document, including, but not limited to, -errors, omissions, or inaccuracies. Because of the rate with which conditions change, the author and publisher reserve the right to alter and update the information contained herein on the new conditions whenever they see applicable.

Table Of Contents

Introduction

I want to thank you and congratulate you for purchasing the book, *"Bikini Competition: Ultimate Bikini Competition Diet Cookbook! – Bikini Competitors Guide With Carb Cycling And Clean Eating Recipes To Prepare And Win Your Bikini Fitness Competition"*

This "Bikini Competition" book contains proven steps and strategies on how to win your bikini fitness competition with the right kind of diet.

Joining a bikini competition is a lot more than looking sexy in a bikini. It takes a lot of self-discipline and control to be able to look fit in time for the competition. You need to understand the different kinds of diet plan that you can try to keep your body fit and toned. This book contains a brief background about popular diet plans such as carb cycling, clean eating, and Paleo. You will also find simple recipes that you can try at home.

You can get some tips and information about bikini competitions and what the judges look for when judging the contestants. This will at least give you an idea what to improve on and what to avoid before joining the competition. You will also learn about different supplements that you can take before the competition to maintain your fit and toned physique.

Finally, this book will also give you some tips and techniques to keep your motivation high that can help you win the competition. After all, it is important that both your mind and body are in excellent condition if you want to be declared as the winner.

Thanks again for purchasing this book, I hope you enjoy it!

Chapter 1: Introduction To Bikini Competition

If you are planning to join a bikini competition, then you should at least learn a thing or two about it to help you perform better during the competition.

Bikini competition used to be a category of fitness and figure competition for women that puts more emphasis on muscularity. Fitness and figure competition is a cross between gymnastics and female bodybuilding and was introduced in 1985 by Wally Boyko during the time when female bodybuilding's popularity stated to decline both in terms of number of contestants and fans. This is because a lot of women do not want to have the physique of a female body builder. For most women, their ideal body type is lean and firm, not manly and bulky. Women want to look fit and toned yet sexy and feminine especially in revealing outfits like the bikini. They do not want to look like a man in a skimpy bikini.

Although muscle definition is emphasized in fitness and figure competition more than muscle size, a lot of women still did not like the idea of building muscles more than they have to. Moreover, the competition has a performance component that is suitable for athletes and gymnasts, but not for a lot of people who have a great physique but are not too athletic. To solve this problem, bikini competition was added as a category to the fitness and figure competition. Bikini competition was only recognized as an independent physique competition in November 7, 2010, the year when the first Bikini Olympia was held. Instead of bulging muscles, the competition looks for lean and firm musculature. It has since become popular especially among women who know that they look amazing wearing a bikini.

Before joining a bikini competition, you need to know the following things that can help you do the necessary preparations.

Determine how long you need to get ready

It is important that you know how much time you will need to get ready for the bikini competition. You can ask a judge, a coach, or a bikini competition participant about this. For instance, diet plans can range from six to 20 plus weeks, assuming that you already have a lean body. If you are a bikini competitor, then you should aim for 8-13% body fat. Female athletes have about 14-21% body fat and an average American woman has 25-31% body fat. You need to reach this level before the competition. This is the best way to determine how long you need to prepare for the competition.

Aside from the physical aspect, you also need to prepare mentally and emotionally. If you have problems or issues and you need to take some time to cope or move on, then you also need to consider this during the preparation. You have to be in a great mood if you want to win.

Set aside enough budget

Participating in a bikini competition can get expensive. You need to pay for the contest prep coach ($200 per month), personal trainer ($50-$100 per session), bikini (off the rack costs $150, customized costs $600-$1000), tanning ($50), shoes ($50), posing coach ($20-$50 per hour), and supplements and special diet meals. Of course, there are ways to save money by finding inexpensive alternatives, but this is the general idea of how much you need to spend when joining a bikini competition.

Manage your expectations

This is an especially important tip for beginners. For beginners, you need to set realistic expectations for yourself. Your main goal for joining your very first bikini competition should be to gain valuable experience that can help you win future competitions. You should be satisfied that you were able to meet the standards to be able to become a bikini competitor. Just look at it as a sweet bonus if you get an award or win the prize.

Competitions are public

If you experience stage fright every time you go on stage, then you should think twice before joining a bikini competition where you have to parade on the stage in front of a large crowd wearing a skimpy outfit. This is also an important consideration if you have a sensitive job, like teacher or public official.

Chapter 2: What The Judges Are Looking For

If you think joining a bikini competition is as simple as looking hot in a bikini, then you are wrong. Note that it is a complicated physique competition that requires a lot more than looking hot in a bikini. You need to know what the judges want that can help you win the competition.

The scoring system may be confusing for a lot of people. Some spectators who watch the competition sometimes wonder if the judges are using a set of standard criteria to judge the competitors because of the scores. They have no clue why the judges like a certain contestant whom the audience does not really care for,but give low scores to the crowd's favorite.

Everyone knows that bikini competitors have lean and fit physique, which is a result of strict diet and exercise regimens. The basic criteria for scoring a bikini competition are physique, symmetry, presentation, posing and stage presence. However, the judges also look at the contestant's confidence and overall marketability.

To give you a better idea about how the judging works in a bikini competition, you can check out the following paragraphs.

Your Physique

The main criterion for judging in bikini contests is the physique. Judges look at the overall physique of the contestant, which includes symmetry, proportion, shape, balance, and skin tone. The contestant should have the "total package". It is important to have a firm and lean physique, but not too muscular that will make you look like a bodybuilder. The muscles should not have visible striations and should show the distinct muscle groups, but not bulging. You will be deducted points if you are too hard, lean and muscular.

You need to have well-developed shoulders and glutes and achieve an hourglass shape to get additional points. This will make your torso look longer and leaner and will make your waist look tinier. To put it in simpler terms, you need to showcase a curvy silhouette with firm muscles and a statuesque figure. You can achieve this if you get the required body fat for bikini competitors.

The Presentation

Aside from having the ideal physique for a bikini competitor, you also need to know how to present yourself on stage. This involves posing and the way you carry yourself. This is what sets bikini competitors apart from other participants of physique competitions. This is where subjectivity in judging enters the picture. When you walk onstage, it is essential that you command the attention of the judges and the crowd from start to finish. Keep in mind that the judges will be looking at your every move and will be taking notes. It is best to give them something that will make them want to give you a high score.

You will have mandatory poses where you need to stand in such a way that will showcase your physique in the most flattering way. You will also have to perform a mandatory front pose where you have to put your weight on one leg, place one hand on your hip, and leave the other hand on the side. You will also be required to do a back pose where you have to look behind your shoulder, position your hips, and toss your hair to attract the judges.

You need to have the right pose, but it is also important to have the right facial expression, accessories, outfit, hair, makeup and tan. Just be sure not to overdo any of these things because the main focus should still be in your physique. Do not distract the judges by wearing an embellished bikini or an elaborate hairstyle and makeup. Your skin should be smooth and silky. It should not have any signs of cellulite because they are looking for toned and firm skin.

The remaining chapters in this book will provide you with some special diet plans and recipes that you can try to help you achieve a lean and firm body before joining a bikini competition.

Chapter 3: Bikini Competition Diet Cookbook Outline

Before joining a bikini competition, it is important to achieve the 8-13% body fat to ensure that your muscles are well defined and you do not have any ounce of visible fats and cellulites in your body. You can achieve this by going on a special diet. You can try any forms of diet such as Paleo, clean eating and carb cycling. You can choose any one of these or a combination of these three. It is important to talk it out with a nutritionist to ensure which kind of diet plan suits you the best. You need the help of an expert when transitioning from an eat-anything-you-like kind of diet to a strict diet regimen that will help you lose fat effectively.

Any serious bikini competitor has a diet plan outline that she follows to ensure that everything she eats is good for her physique. Below is a basic bikini competition diet cookbook outline that you can use as a guide when creating your own meal plans.

Master Food List

This can help you make the best food choices when trying to lose fat and gain muscles. You can substitute other foods that are not in the list as long as they provide the necessary nutrient and the right amount of calories.

1. *Protein*
Fish – frozen or fresh tuna, cod, tilapia, salmon, snapper; canned tuna

Turkey – ground lean turkey breast

Beef – ground lean beef cuts like sirloin steak, filet, flank, and round

Chicken breast- ground white chicken breast; frozen or fresh chicken breast without bones and skin; baked or rotisserie whole chicken breasts without skin

2. *Vegetables (non-starchy)*

Asparagus, Cauliflower, Celery, Spinach, Cucumbers, Onions, Summer squash, Tomatoes, All varieties of peppers, All varieties of lettuce, Green beans

3. Fruits
Apples, Berries like blueberries, raspberries, and strawberries, Cantaloupe, Fresh peaches, Oranges, Pears, Pineapples, Grapefruit, Bananas

4. Starchy carbohydrates
Yams or sweet potatoes, Brown rice, Beans such as kidney, lima, and black, White and red potatoes, Oatmeal

5. Fats
Almonds and walnuts, Cashew, peanut, or almond butter, Heavy whipping cream, Olive, flaxseed, and safflower oil

6. Beverages
Water, Sparkling water, coffee, diet soda, tea

7. Others
Dry seasoning, salt, sugar-free gum, vinegar, mustard, citrus peels, lemon or lime juice, sugar-free Jell-O

Meals

You should eat 4 to 5 times a day every 4 or 5 hours. Your last meal should be at least a couple of hours before bedtime. Your meals should consist of two protein shakes with 3 regular meals.

1. **Breakfast** – 1 small serving of protein, 1 serving of complex carbohydrates, and 1 serving of vegetables.
2. **Mid-morning snack** – protein drink/shake
3. **Lunch** – 1 medium serving of protein, 2 to 3 servings of vegetables
4. **Mid afternoon snack** – protein drink/shake
5. **Dinner** – 1 large serving of protein, 2 to 3 servings of vegetables, 1 serving of fat (for the dressing)

You have to make sure that your every meal has all the recommended nutrients that your body needs to help you achieve 8-13% body fat in time for the competition.

Chapter 4: Carb Cycling Diet For Bikini Competitors

You have probably heard of the popular low carb diet wherein you are required to lower your consumption of carbohydrates to achieve weight loss. Some people criticize the low carb diet because our body needs carbohydrates that serve as the body's fuel. You cannot simply give up or lower your carbohydrate consumption especially if you are working out. Eating a lot of protein-rich foods is not enough because protein cannot provide all the energy that your body needs since its main function is for muscle building. This is why experts and personal trainers came up with a solution by devising a diet plan called the carb cycling diet.

The main principle of the carb cycling diet is to eat high-carb, moderate-carb, and no/low carb alternately throughout the week. You are required to eat high protein foods the whole week. Your fat intake is highly dependent on your carbohydrate intake. Your fat is low if you consume high carb foods and vice versa.

The basic structure of the carb cycling diet varies, but all of them have the same effect on your body. For instance, you can have 4 days of low-carb meals, 1 day of high-carb, and 1 day of no carb, then repeat the same structure. You can also start with three low-carb days, 1 high-carb, then start over.

So how can you distinguish no/low-carb, moderate-carb, and high-carb from each other? You need to eat 2 to 2.5 grams of carb for every pound of your weight to have a high-carb day. Your protein and fat intake per pound of weight should be 1 gram and 0 to .15 gram, respectively. For your moderate-carb day, you need to consume 1.5 grams of carb for every pound of weight. Your fat consumption will be around 0.2 gram and your protein consumption around 1 to 1.2 grams for every pound of weight.

On low-carb days, you need to eat at around 0.5 gram of carb for every pound of weight, with 1.5 grams of protein and 0.35 grams of fat for each pound. No-carb day does not necessarily mean you should have 0-carbohydrate intake because this is almost impossible to achieve. A no-carb day only means consuming not more than 30 grams of carb per day. Protein will be around 1.5 grams and fat will be around 0.5 to 0.8 gram per pound of body weight.

Chapter 5: Carb Cycling Recipes For Bikini Competitors

Sirloin Steak with Tomatoes and Green Beans

Ingredients:

6 oz sirloin steak, lean and boneless

1 cup green beans

1 tomato, chopped

1 spritz of olive oil

¾ tsp garlic

Salt and pepper

Instructions:

1. Spritz olive oil on nonstick pan. Cook meat on both sides on high heat. Transfer meat to plate and set aside.
2. Cook the green beans for about 3 minutes on medium heat. Toss in garlic and cook for another minute. Add salt and pepper according to desired flavor.
3. Cook chopped tomatoes for about 1 minute. Let the vegetables cook in a covered pan for about 4 minutes or until the tomatoes produce their natural juices.
4. Serve the vegetables with the sirloin steak.
5. You can serve this with avocado to make it a low-carb meal or baked potato or brown rice to make it a high-carb meal.

Cauliflower Rice

Ingredients:

1 head of cauliflower, chop coarsely to resemble rice

Instructions:

1. Steam chopped cauliflower for about 5 minutes

2. Add low-fat butter or margarine when done.

Lemon Chicken

Ingredients:

2 chicken breasts

¼ cup of lemon juice

1 spritz olive oil

1 tsp garlic, minced

Salt and pepper

Instructions:

1. In a resealable bag, put all the ingredients and seal. Gently massage the contents of the bag to ensure that all the ingredients and their flavors are mixed together. Marinate for at least 30 minutes.
2. Get the meat from the bag and discard the rest of the marinade. Grill chicken on each side over medium-high heat according to desired doneness.
3. Serve with a sliced tomato or side salad with salad dressing to turn it into a low-carb meal. Serve with side salad or veggies and couscous or red potatoes to turn it into a high-carb meal.

Chicken with Garlic, Basil, and Tomato

Ingredients:

2 chicken breasts

1 spritz olive oil

2 tsp garlic, basil, and tomato seasoning

Instructions:

1. Coat both sides of the chicken breast with seasoning.

2. Heat pan with olive oil over medium heat and cook chicken breasts on both sides.

3. Serve with baby spinach or sliced tomatoes sprinkled with the garlic, basil, and tomato seasoning and drizzle with olive oil and balsamic vinegar to make it a low-carb meal.

4. Serve with veggies or side salad and a serving of quinoa, brown rice, or baked potato to make it a high-carb meal.

Banana Almond-Chocolate Protein Shake

Ingredients:

1 cup of unsweetened almond milk in vanilla flavor

1 scoop of whey protein powder n chocolate flavor

½ banana

1 tbsp almond butter

1 cup of ice

Instructions:

Mix all the ingredients together in a blender until the consistency is thick and smooth. Transfer contents to a large glass and enjoy a refreshing protein shake.

Chapter 6: Clean Eating Recipes For Weight Loss

Clean eating does not mean eating foods that are free from dirt. This is a diet plan that involves choosing high quality foods and avoiding junk and processed foods as much as possible. The basic principles of clean eating are listed in the next paragraph.

Principles of clean eating

1. *Eat whole foods.* When you say whole foods, these refer to those that have not undergone artificial processes in the lab or factory. These foods are in their most natural state and are harvested straight from the farm.

2. *Eliminate processed foods.* One way to tell if a food is processed is by checking if there is a label or not. Anything that has a label is most likely processed because it involves more than one ingredient. Clean eating does not mean completely eliminating all processed foods. You can still eat natural cheeses and whole grain pasta even though they are considered processed.

3. *Avoid refined sugar.* Avoid anything refined because the food no longer has its original nutrients after undergoing the process designed to make it more palatable or give it a longer shelf life.

4. *Combine carbs with protein or fat.* This is the perfect formula for bikini competitors. This will provide you with the energy you need and will help you develop muscles and lose fat.

5. *Eat small, frequent meals.* Clean eating also requires you to eat smaller meals more frequently. You can eat three regular meals and two snacks in between. Some even eat as many as six small meals a day to prevent hunger pangs.

Clean eating recipes

Here are some clean eating recipes that you can try at home.

Classic Tomato and Cucumber Salad

Ingredients:

2 cups cherry or grape tomatoes, sliced in half

2 medium sized cucumbers, peeled and sliced thinly

½ of red onion, sliced thinly

2 tbsp balsamic vinegar

2 tbsp fresh dill

1 tbsp olive oil

1 tsp pure maple syrup or honey

1 tsp Dijon mustard

Salt and pepper

Instructions:

1. Mix all the tomatoes, cucumbers, and onions in a large mixing bowl. In another smaller bowl, combine the rest of the ingredients using a whisk.
2. Pour the dressing over the vegetables and toss all the ingredients together to coat.
3. Serve right away.

Roasted Pear Sandwich and Baby Spinach

Ingredients:

2 pcs of pears, peeled, cored, and sliced thinly

1 cup of baby spinach

4 slices of artisan bread, whole grain and cut horizontally

2 tsp of canola oil

1 tsp of lemon juice, freshly squeezed

Instructions:

1. Preheat oven at 400 degrees F.

2. In a medium bowl, mix together lemon juice and canola oil.
3. Toss in the sliced pears until well coated with the oil and lemon juice. Put the pears on a baking sheet and bake until they become golden and tender, which takes about 20 minutes.
4. Toast your bread slices and apply your favorite spread on one side of each bread slice. Add the pears and spinach and gently press the bread slices together.

Chapter 7: Paleo Diet For Bikini Competitors

Another diet plan that you can try if you plan to join a bikini competition is the Paleo diet, which is short for Paleolithic diet. This diet is based on the dietary history of humans. In a nutshell, Paleo diet is eating the food that our ancestors ate thousands of years ago. People who lived thousands of years ago were not affected by chronic illnesses that result from unhealthy eating habits and lifestyle. You need to understand that Paleo diet, just like clean eating diet, is a lot more than a diet plan. It is also a kind of lifestyle that requires healthy changes in different aspects of your life.

Some of the basic principles of the Paleo diet are as follows:

Eat whole, natural foods

As explained earlier, whole foods are foods that are in their most natural state. Foods that are harvested directly from the farm retain their complete nutrients. Moreover, your body is less likely to reject whole foods because they do not have any artificial ingredients. Paleo diet encourages you to eat fresh produce that came straight from the ground or fresh meat.

Limit your consumption of processed and refined foods

Our ancestors did not eat anything that has been processed in a laboratory or factory because there were no such facilities at that time. Processed or refined foods are stripped off their nutrients. You may be eating vegetables; but if they are processed, then you are still not getting the complete nutrients that you should be getting if you eat them fresh. You need to avoid anything that has a label because these food items are most likely processed or refined. Some examples of refined foods are cereals, pastas, or breads or anything made of flour. You should also avoid eating dairy products and sugary drinks and foods as much as you can. If you really have to eat them, be sure to limit your consumption of these food items to the minimum amount.

Choose your meat, poultry, and fish carefully

You are allowed to eat meat in Paleo diet, but be sure that the meat is grass-fed and not grain-fed. You can also eat any kind of fowl like chicken, turkey, or duck. Be sure to buy wild fish because toxins such as mercury can be a problem with farmed fish.

So basically, the foods that you can eat in Paleo include fresh produce like fruits and vegetables, sea foods, lean meats, nuts and seeds, and healthy fats. You should avoid eating grains, dairy products, legumes, starches, processed foods and sugars, and alcohol. You can find alternatives to ensure that you are still following the Paleo diet.

Chapter 8: Paleo Diet Recipes

Bacon Avocado Omelets

Ingredients:

1 avocado

4 slices of bacon

4 eggs

2 tbsp red onion, minced

1 tbsp fresh cilantro, minced

1 dash of hot sauce

Instructions:

1. Fry bacon in hot oil until crisp.
2. Cut your avocado vertically in half and get rid of the pit. Using a spoon, scoop out the flesh and put it in a bowl. Mash it up a little, but not too much because you still want to have a little texture. You can do these while the bacon is cooking.
3. Toss in the cilantro and onion in the avocado.
4. Drain the bacon in paper towels to remove excess oil. Snip or crumble the bacon and add the pieces to your avocado mixture.
5. Using your eggs, start making the omelets by adding the avocado mixture. You can top it off with hot sauce if you like it hot and spicy.

Chicken Salad

Ingredients:

1 cup of cooked chicken, diced

1 heart of cooked artichoke, chopped

½ cup of red bell pepper, diced

2 scallions, thinly sliced

1 tbsp of fresh parsley, minced

1/3 cup of balsamic-lemon mayo

Instructions:

1. Put all the sliced vegetables in a large bowl.
2. Add the mayo to the vegetables and toss until they are well-coated.

Asian Shrimp with Pepper

Ingredients:

1 and ½ pounds of raw shrimp, peeled

4 cloves of garlic, crushed

3 tbsp of coconut oil

1 tbsp of coconut aminos

¼ cup of fresh cilantro, chopped

1 tsp of black pepper

1 tbsp of fish sauce

Instructions:

1. Heat coconut oil in a skillet and add the crushed garlic cloves. Cook for about 2 to 3 minutes, stirring, over low heat. Do not brown the garlic.
2. Toss in the raw shrimp and cook with the garlic until the shrimp turns pink. This will take about 4 to 5 minutes. Add the fish sauce, coconut aminos, and black pepper and cook for another minute. Transfer the shrimp on a plate and let the remaining liquid cook for another minute or two over medium heat. Pour this liquid on the cooked shrimp.
3. Serve the shrimp with chopped fresh cilantro and serve.

Walnut-Apple Coleslaw

Ingredients:

1 apple, cored and sliced into strips

½ cup of walnuts, chopped

4 cups of cabbage, shredded

2 tbsp of mayo

2 tbsp of apple cider vinegar

3 tbsp of walnut oil

¼ tsp of Dijon mustard

¼ tsp of black pepper

Salt

Instructions:

1. Preheat over at 350 degrees F.
2. Place walnuts on a baking tin and bake for 8 minutes.
3. While walnuts are baking, put the shredded cabbage and apple strips in a mixing bowl. Toss the rest of the ingredients in the bowl.
4. After 8 minutes, the walnuts should be toasty. If not, bake them for another 2 minutes before tossing them in with the rest of the ingredients.
5. Add your dressing and mix all the ingredients to coat the apples and cabbages well.

Chapter 9: Supplements For Bikini Competition

Aside from having a healthy diet and lifestyle, bikini competitors also have to take supplements to get all the nutrients that their body needs. Here are some of the most common supplements that most bikini competitors take.

Multivitamins

Whether you are trying to lose, gain, or maintain weight, you need to take multivitamins that will serve as a strong foundation for your body. It is important that you get complete nutrition every day for your overall health.

BCAA

This stands for Branched Chain Amino Acids that are composed of three essential amino acids namely valine, isoleucine, and leucine. One third of your muscle tissues are composed of these three amino acids, which makes BCAA good for muscle building, energy and recuperation.

ZMA

This stands for Zinc Monomethionine Aspartate, which contains Vitamin B6, Magnesium and Zinc. This helps maximize tissue repair while you sleep.

Glutamine

Another essential amino acid in the body, glutamine helps you gain lean muscle and boost your immune system. Your body loses its natural glutamine as you exercise, which is why it is important to take glutamine supplements.

Fish oil

This is an important supplement for bikini competitors because it helps build muscle and lose fat. It is also good for your overall health and wellbeing. This supplement is obtained from some fatty fish like mackerel, salmon, and krill.

Creatine

Creatine is a supplement that has been used by workout buffs and bodybuilders and can also be used by bikini competitors. It helps improve muscle power, strength and speed of movements.

Green tea extract

Although not necessarily required, most physique competitors take green tea extract to improve their metabolism. It also contains antioxidants that can improve your overall health. Taking green tea extract is different from drinking green tea extract gas, which has more catechins and EGCG, common types of antioxidants.

Chapter 10: How To Keep Motivation High And Win!

Winning a bikini competition takes a lot more than eating healthy. You also need to have the right mindset that will help you win. You need to boost your confidence if you want to win any competition. To boost your confidence, you need to be well prepared so that you know that you have done the best that you could in time for the competition. You should also focus on your assets instead of wasting your time focusing on the things that you cannot change.

Another way to boost your motivation is to keep your focus. You need to set your sight on tangible goals that you will enjoy. For example, instead of simply focusing on winning the competition, you can focus on the prize money that will help you buy things that you want or go on your dream vacation. You can also focus on having your ideal body. By developing a tangible focus, it is easier for you to see the purpose behind your desire to win the competition.

Another way to keep your motivation high and to win is to have a mentor or a buddy who can help you on your journey towards achieving your ideal physique. It is important to find a coach or a trainer whom you can look up to as your mentor or a workout buddy who will also join the bikini competition. Having someone who understands the trials and tribulations of joining a bikini competition will help keep your motivation high especially during difficult times when you feel like giving up.

Finally, the best motivation of all is knowing that you will not only have a lean and fit body that most women envy, but also a healthy life that is free from sickness and illnesses.

Conclusion

Thank you again for purchasing the book Bikini Competition information and cookbook!

I am extremely excited to pass this information along to you, and I am so happy that you now have read and can hopefully implement these strategies going forward.

I hope this book was able to help you understand the different diets that you can try when joining a bikini competition and how they can help you achieve your ideal physique.

The next step is to get started using this information and to hopefully live a healthier life!

Please don't be someone who just reads this information and doesn't apply it, the strategies in this book will only benefit you if you use them!

If you know of anyone else that could benefit from the information presented here please inform them of this book.

Finally, if you enjoyed this book and feel it has added value to your life in any way, please take the time to share your thoughts and post a review on Amazon. It'd be greatly appreciated!

Thank you and good luck!

Preview Of:

The Clean Eating Ultimate Cookbook And Diet Guide!

<u>Clean Eating</u>

Low Fat, Paleo, And Low Carb Recipes For Maximum Weight Loss And To Boost Your Metabolism For Fast Results!

Introduction

I want to thank you and congratulate you for purchasing the book, *"Clean Eating: The Clean Eating Ultimate Cookbook And Diet Guide! – Low Fat, Paleo, And Low Carb Recipes For Maximum Weight Loss And To Boost Your Metabolism For Fast Results!"*

This book contains proven steps and strategies on how to lose weight and boost your metabolism as quickly as possible based on the principles of clean eating and using popular diet recipes like low fat, paleo, and low carb recipes.

These days, you need to be more mindful of the kinds of food that you eat. You have to make sure that what you are eating is as natural as possible to provide you with the essential nutrients that your body needs without worrying about side effects or acquiring diseases. People these days choose convenience over health by buying processed and ready-to-eat foods that do not contribute much to your health. In this fast paced world where fast food and instant meals are popular, you have to be more disciplined with the meals that you cook not only for yourself but also for your whole family.

This book will give you some basic facts and background on the principles of clean eating and different kinds of diet plans and strategies like low fat, paleo, low carb, carb cycling, flexible, and IIFYM. You can also find some tips on how to lose maximum weight, boost your metabolism, and get in shape. To get you started on your clean eating diet plan, you can use the recipes provided in the last few chapters of this book.

Thanks again for purchasing this book, I hope you enjoy it!

Chapter 1: Clean Eating Cookbook And Diet Guide

You have probably heard of clean eating from one of your health conscious or diet enthusiast friends. If not, you are probably asking the question that many people are asking, what exactly is clean eating? The main concept of clean eating is eating foods at their most natural state. This includes foods that are raw, fresh, and unprocessed. It is not just about the quantity but more on the quality of food that you eat. Clean eating is not just a diet fad or trend. It is a sound approach to healthy living through eating the right kinds of food that gives you the energy you need and makes you a healthier individual.

If you are going to adopt clean eating in your lifestyle, you need to understand its basic principles.

Eat whole and natural foods

Whole and natural foods are foods that have not been processed and are usually packed in a box, can, and plastic packaging. A bag of fresh beans may be packed in a plastic bag but this does not mean that these beans are not whole or natural. It is important that the foods that you eat are fresh or are in their most natural state, which means less cooking and very little processing, if at all.

Add fat, carbohydrate, and protein to your diet

Good fat and carbohydrate are essential minerals and they are easy to get from the usual foods that you eat everyday like grains, oil, pasta, and so on. However, many people lack protein in their diet, especially breakfast. It is important to get the right amount of protein that your body needs to help develop your muscles and also make you feel full longer.

Eat small meals frequently

The clean eating diet advises you to eat about five to six small meals in a day. This includes the usual breakfast, lunch, and dinner, plus two to three snacks in between meals. By eating small meals frequently, you will not go hungry easily which can often lead to overeating or eating just about anything you can grab. The small meals throughout the day also help stabilize the level of sugar in your bloodstream which prevents energy lag.

Drink at least two liters of water per day

This will keep your body hydrated which will prevent you from feeling tired. Avoid high calorie drinks like soda or energy drink because you need to get your calories from the food that you eat and not your drinks. It is also important to use a reusable canteen rather than plastic.

Learn how to read labels

Clean eating requires you to learn how to read labels because this is where you will find the ingredients. If the list of ingredients contain long names that are difficult to pronounce, this could mean that it has an artificial ingredient which is banned from clean eating.

Thanks For Previewing My Exciting Book Entitled:

"Clean Eating: The Clean Eating Ultimate Cookbook And Diet Guide! Low Fat, Paleo, And Low Carb Recipes For Maximum Weight Loss And To Boost Your Metabolism For Fast Results!"

To purchase this book, simply go to the Amazon Kindle store and simply search:

"CLEAN EATING"

Then just scroll down until you see my book. You will know it is mine because you will see my name "Sarah Brooks" underneath the title.

Alternatively, you can visit my author page on Amazon to see this book and other work I have done. Thanks so much, and please don't forget your free bonuses to find it.

DON'T LEAVE YET! - CHECK OUT YOUR FREE BONUSES BELOW!

Free Bonus Offer: Get Free Access To The <u>LiveFitVIP.com</u> VIP Newsletter!

Once you enter your email address you will immediately get free access to this awesome newsletter!

But wait, right now if you join now for free you will also get free access to the "The 7 Keys To Body Transformation" free EBook!

To claim both your FREE VIP NEWSLETTER MEMBERSHIP and your FREE BONUS Ebook on THE 7 KEYS TO BODY TRANSFORMATION!

<u>Just Go To:</u>

<u>www.liveFitVIP.com</u>

70934936R10020

Made in the USA
San Bernardino, CA
09 March 2018